**LET'S TALK
ABOUT: HEALTH**

I am a clinical social worker supporting sexual health and reproductive psychology.

9 781312 744769

Date:_____

_____

Where were you born?

_____

_____

_____

_____

_____

_____

_____

_____

_____

_____

_____

_____

_____

_____

_____

_____

_____

Where did you grow up?

_____
_____
_____
_____
_____
_____
_____
_____
_____
_____
_____
_____
_____
_____
_____
_____
_____
_____

Date:_____

_____

What were your parents jobs?

_____
_____
_____
_____
_____
_____
_____
_____
_____
_____
_____
_____
_____
_____
_____
_____

_____

What was your first job?

_____
_____
_____
_____
_____
_____
_____
_____
_____
_____
_____
_____
_____
_____
_____
_____
_____
_____

_____

What jobs have you had?

_____

_____

_____

_____

_____

_____

_____

_____

_____

_____

_____

_____

_____

_____

_____

What types of things did you like to do before you had kids?

_____

_____

_____

_____

_____

_____

_____

_____

_____

_____

_____

_____

_____

_____

_____

_____

_____

_____

Date:_____

_____

Tell me about a favorite memory from when you were raising your family.

_____

_____

_____

_____

_____

_____

_____

_____

_____

_____

_____

_____

_____

_____

_____

_____

_____

_____

What is your all-time favorite movie?

_____

_____

_____

_____

_____

_____

_____

_____

_____

_____

_____

_____

_____

_____

_____

_____

_____

_____

Date: _____

_____

What did you do after high school?

_____
_____
_____
_____
_____
_____
_____
_____
_____
_____
_____
_____
_____
_____
_____
_____
_____

Did you play any sports or were you in any activities in high school?

_____

_____

_____

_____

_____

_____

_____

_____

_____

_____

_____

_____

_____

_____

_____

_____

_____

_____

Date: _____

_____

Tell me about a time you got into trouble when you were
a kid.

_____

_____

_____

_____

_____

_____

_____

_____

_____

_____

_____

_____

_____

_____

_____

_____

_____

Did you have a favorite teacher or subject in school?

_____
_____
_____
_____
_____
_____
_____
_____
_____
_____
_____
_____
_____
_____
_____
_____
_____

Date:_____

_____

What did you do for fun as a kid?

_____
_____
_____
_____
_____
_____
_____
_____
_____
_____
_____
_____
_____
_____
_____
_____

Date: _____

_____

How did you spend holidays as a child?

_____
_____
_____
_____
_____
_____
_____
_____
_____
_____
_____
_____
_____
_____
_____
_____
_____
_____
_____

_____

Did you have any pets as a child?

_____
_____
_____
_____
_____
_____
_____
_____
_____
_____
_____
_____
_____
_____
_____
_____
_____
_____

Date:_____

Tell me about the town/city you grew up in.

_____

_____

_____

_____

_____

_____

_____

_____

_____

_____

_____

_____

_____

_____

_____

_____

_____

_____

_____

_____

Tell me about your siblings.

_____

_____

_____

_____

_____

_____

_____

_____

_____

_____

_____

_____

_____

_____

_____

_____

_____

Who did you admire or look up to when you were growing up?

Date: _____

_____

What was your childhood home like?

_____
_____
_____
_____
_____
_____
_____
_____
_____
_____
_____
_____
_____
_____
_____
_____
_____

_____

Did you have a nickname as a child?

_____

_____

_____

_____

_____

_____

_____

_____

_____

_____

_____

_____

_____

_____

_____

_____

_____

_____

_____

Date: _____

_____

What are some of your favorite childhood
memories?

_____

_____

_____

_____

_____

_____

_____

_____

_____

_____

_____

_____

_____

_____

_____

_____

_____

_____

_____

Who was your best friend when you were a kid?

_____
_____
_____
_____
_____
_____
_____
_____
_____
_____
_____
_____
_____
_____
_____
_____
_____
_____
_____
_____

Date:_____

_____

Tell me a favorite memory about your parents.

_____

_____

_____

_____

_____

_____

_____

_____

_____

_____

_____

_____

_____

_____

_____

_____

_____

_____

Date:_____

_____

Tell me about your grandparents.

_____
_____
_____
_____
_____
_____
_____
_____
_____
_____
_____
_____
_____
_____
_____
_____
_____
_____
_____

_____

Tell me about your extended family.

_____

_____

_____

_____

_____

_____

_____

_____

_____

_____

_____

_____

_____

_____

_____

_____

_____

_____

What is something that has helped you through difficult times?

_____

_____

_____

_____

_____

_____

_____

_____

_____

_____

_____

_____

_____

_____

_____

_____

_____

_____

Date: _____

_____

Tell me something you've done that you are really proud of.

_____
_____
_____
_____
_____
_____
_____
_____
_____
_____
_____
_____
_____
_____
_____
_____
_____
_____
_____

Have you ever done something you didn't think you could do?

_____

What do you love best about being a grandparent?

_____

_____

_____

_____

_____

_____

_____

_____

_____

_____

_____

_____

_____

_____

_____

Date:_____

_____

Do you have a favorite quote or scripture passage?

_____

_____

_____

_____

_____

_____

_____

_____

_____

_____

_____

_____

_____

_____

_____

_____

_____

_____

What is one of the hardest things you've ever had to do?

_____

_____

_____

_____

_____

_____

_____

_____

_____

_____

_____

_____

_____

_____

_____

_____

_____

Date:_____

What is your favorite song?
What is your favorite book?

_____

_____

_____

_____

_____

_____

_____

_____

_____

_____

_____

_____

_____

_____

_____

_____

_____

_____

TRAVEL JOURNAL

where are some places you
have enjoyed traveling?

tell me about your
family tree

Title:

Name	
Date of Birth	Photograph Here
Location of Birth	
Date of Death	
Location of Death	
Mother	
Father	
Spouse(s)	**Notes**
Children	

Title:

Name	
Date of Birth	Photograph Here
Location of Birth	
Date of Death	
Location of Death	
Mother	
Father	**Notes**
Spouse(s)	
Children	

Title:

Name	
Date of Birth	*Photograph Here*
Location of Birth	
Date of Death	
Location of Death	
Mother	
Father	**Notes**
Spouse(s)	
Children	

Title:

Name	
Date of Birth	
Location of Birth	Photograph Here
Date of Death	
Location of Death	
Mother	
Father	
Spouse(s)	**Notes**
Children	

GENERATIONAL FAMILY TREE

NAME BY: _____

DATE : _____

Genealogy

NAME: ## Organizer

DATE OF BIRTH:

DATE OF BIRTH:

FATHER

MOTHER

SPOUSES

CHILDREN

NOTE

Genealogy
Organizer

NAME:

DATE OF BIRTH:

DATE OF BIRTH:

FATHER

MOTHER

SPOUSES

CHILDREN

NOTE

Family Research

TIME: _____ DATE: _____

ANCESTOR : ....

....

TOPICS : ....

....

I KNOW THAT : ....

....

....

....

MY INFORMATION SOURCES : ....

....

....

ACTION PLAN : ....

....

....

....

NOTE
....
....
....
....

Family Research

TIME: DATE:

ANCESTOR : ....
....

TOPICS : ....
....

I KNOW THAT : ....
....
....
....

MY INFORMATION SOURCES : ....
....
....

ACTION PLAN : ....
....
....
....

NOTE
....
....
....
....

Family Group Sheet

FAMILY NAME: _____   **SHEET:** _____

HUSBAND

FATHER   ### MOTHER

BRITH DATE: _____ PLACE: _____ BAPTISED: _____

MARRIAGE: _____ PLACE: _____

DEATH: _____ PLACE: _____ BURIAL: _____

....

....

WIFE

FATHER   ### MOTHER

BRITH DATE: _____ PLACE: _____ BAPTISED: _____

MARRIAGE: _____ PLACE: _____

DEATH: _____ PLACE: _____ BURIAL: _____

....

....

CHILDREN

NAME	D.O.B	D.O.B	SPOUSE	D.O.B	D.O.B

Family Group Sheet

FAMILY NAME:	SHEET:

HUSBAND

FATHER   MOTHER

BRITH DATE: PLACE: BAPTISED:

MARRIAGE: PLACE:

DEATH: PLACE: BURIAL:

WIFE

FATHER   MOTHER

BRITH DATE: PLACE: BAPTISED:

MARRIAGE: PLACE:

DEATH: PLACE: BURIAL:

CHILDREN

NAME	D.O.B	D.O.B	SPOUSE	D.O.B	D.O.B

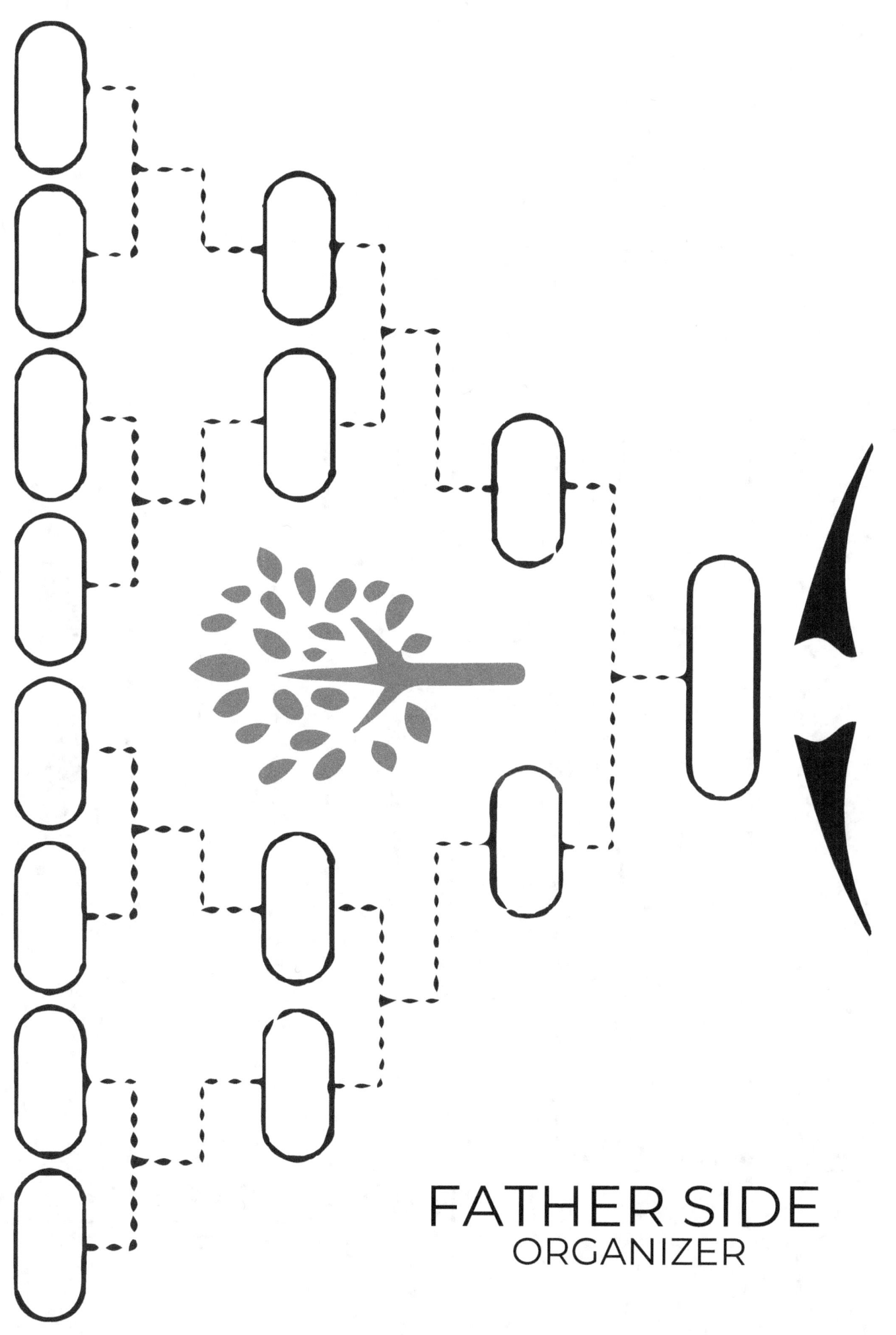

FATHER SIDE
ORGANIZER

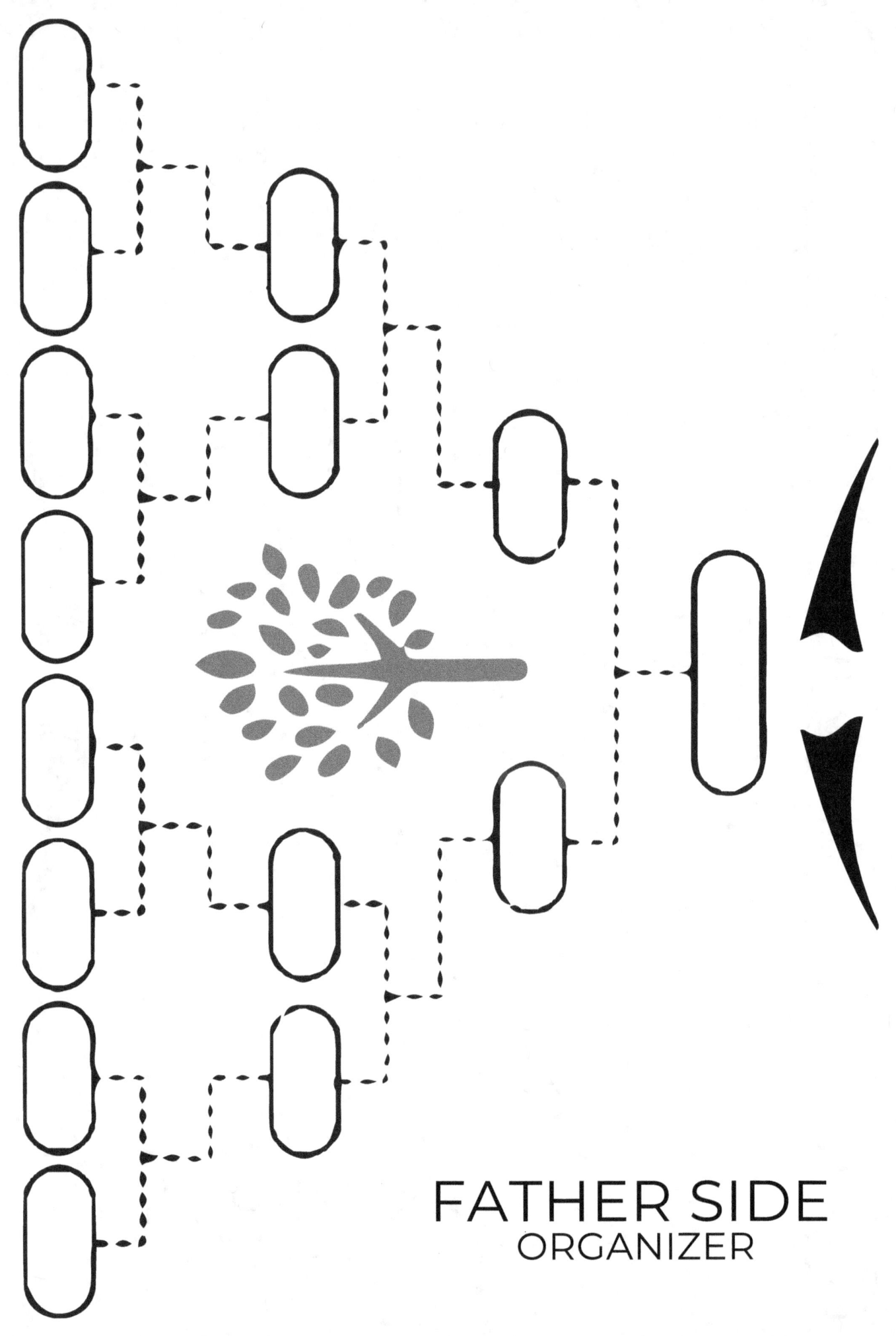

FATHER SIDE
ORGANIZER

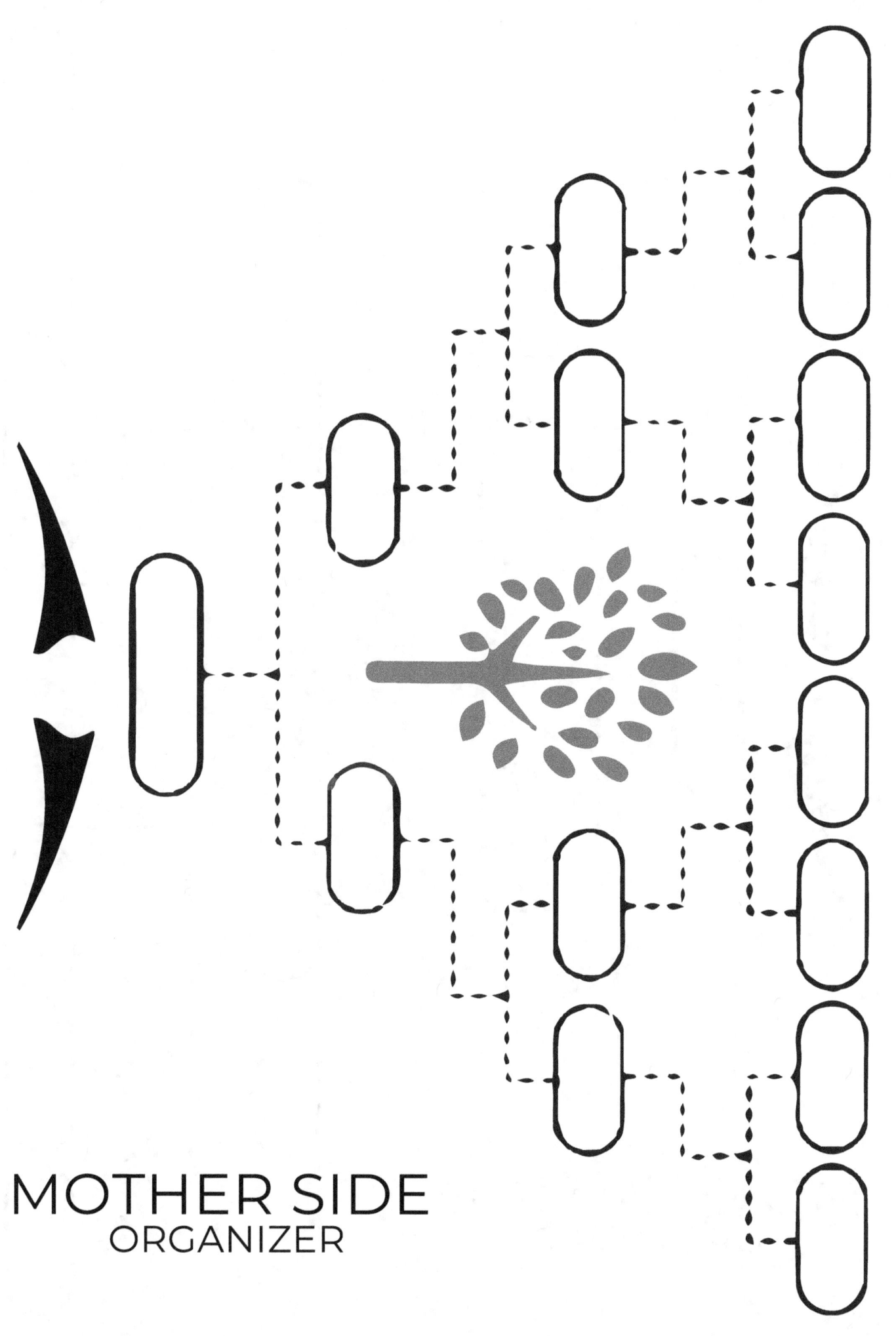

MOTHER SIDE
ORGANIZER

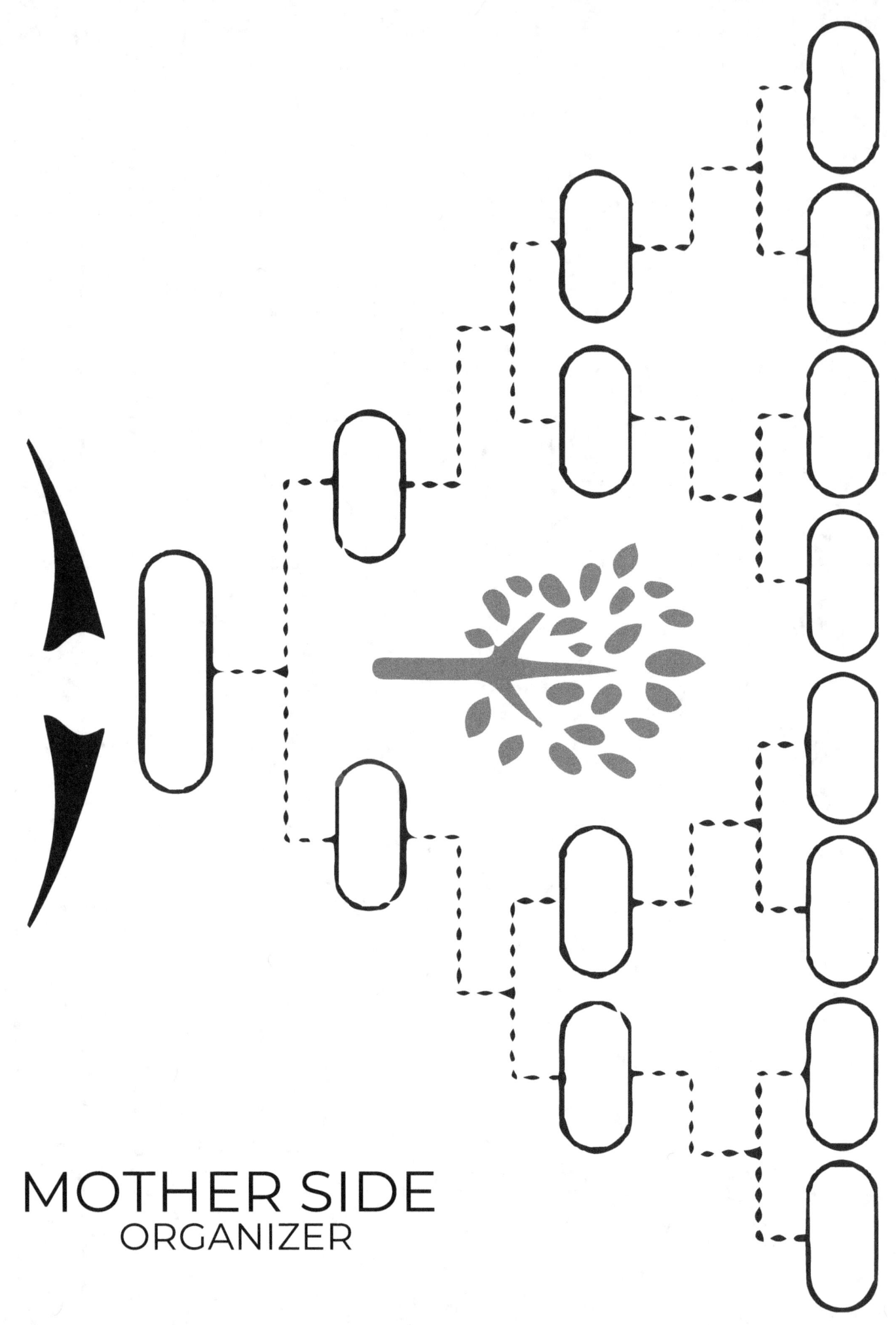

MOTHER SIDE
ORGANIZER

Date:_____

_____

Date:_____

www.ingramcontent.com/pod-product-compliance
Lightning Source LLC
Chambersburg PA
CBHW080446290526
45791CB00008BA/2624